STRONG ENOUGH

Notes on discovering hope, love and strength within

DHIMAN

ISBN: 9798473782776

First published: July 2021

CONTENTS

Strong Enough

Dhiman

INTRODUCTION

No matter what you are going through right now, I hope you will find in these pages something to look forward to, something better than what you have been through. I hope you will rediscover the courage to face your difficult days and find the strength within you to overcome them. Most of all, I hope you will find *hope* again. Even if you are afraid and uncertain right now, remember that you are not alone and your story does not end here.

I hope this book will serve as a reminder for you to believe in yourself, no matter how difficult life gets.

Love,
Dhiman

Strong Enough

Dhiman

HOPE IN THE DIFFICULT

Strong Enough

Dhiman

TO A HEART THAT IS WORRIED

As terrifying and uncertain
as it seems from here,
you will not be stuck
in your struggles forever
you will grow and you will move forward
perhaps not the way you desired
but even in the darkest hours of this journey
you will find reasons to be hopeful.
It might take a little while to get there
and the road ahead might even scare you
but with faith and hope in your heart
you know you will have
something to guide you through.

YOU HAVE WHAT IT TAKES

When your heart aches because the road in front is a dark and unknown one and it makes you worry if this is where all your hopes and dreams are going to end, remember that you have been through lonely paths before and you have felt the same way about the future all those times and still you have conquered them all. So be hopeful that even though it all seems impossible from here, you are strong and you have what it takes to overcome this one and all the ones that will come after.

IF LIFE FEELS TOO HEAVY
TO CARRY ON TODAY
AND YOUR PROGRESS SEEMS
SLOWER THAN YESTERDAY,
REMEMBER THE MOUNTAINS
DID NOT BECOME MOUNTAINS IN ONE DAY.

A S S U R A N C E

I know it still hurts you and I know it wasn't fair on you. You may not know the reason behind everything that has happened to you and maybe you are still wondering if you will ever be able to make it through. But even here as you wander through the unknowns know that something better is waiting for you, trust that despite everything that has happened something good can still happen for you.

IT IS OKAY

It is okay to not know it all,
to do it differently
than what you once thought.
Sometimes life can become too heavy
and I hope you know
it is completely okay
if you cannot carry it any further.
You are free to lay that weight down,
you are allowed to let go
what keeps hurting your heart.

ON THE SEASON OF STRUGGLE

I know it feels like eternity, as if how you feel is never going to change. Perhaps, people tell you it is all in your mind and not true. And I know it hurts you because they don't see the inside and what you are going through. But here's something you can carry in your heart as you move forward: no matter how it feels right now, things in your life will change as they always do. But for now, keep trusting in yourself and the journey in front of you. Have faith in your heart that in your own time you are going to make it through.

WHILE YOU ARE STRIVING TO GET TO
WHERE YOU WANT TO BE SOMEDAY,
MAY YOU BE GRATEFUL
FOR THE PROGRESS
YOU HAVE ALREADY MADE
ALONG THE WAY.

YOU MATTER

Show patience to your heart. Let yourself be reminded that you matter more than what still hurts. Let the difficult days know that even though you are hurting you are still strong enough and you have not given up. Let the darkness that aims to engulf your light know that in your own time you will rise. Let the painful in you be softened by your kindness, compassion and love. It's okay if it takes time, it's okay if you need time. Remember: just because you are struggling today does not mean you are falling behind.

INWARD

When you are afraid
when fear makes you think
giving up is the only way,
remember to look deep into your heart
where hope is still shining bright
telling you that as long as you are here
there is always a way out.

GIVE HOPE ANOTHER CHANCE

Perhaps things that you thought would change this year have not changed. Maybe you feel more worried and stressed than last year. But I hope you know some changes take longer than others. Give hope another chance. This is still a new road for you and it's okay if you need a little more time to learn how to navigate through its twists and turns. Remember – the difficult roads are not here to stay; they are only a part of the journey of a life you truly deserve.

AND EVEN THOUGH
THIS SEASON HAS CHANGED
A LOT OF THINGS,
YOU ARE STILL HERE,
WALKING AT YOUR OWN PACE
ALONG THIS BEAUTIFUL JOURNEY OF
BECOMING.

GROWING IN STRENGTH

Perhaps it seems a little uncertain from here and you are afraid of moving forward. But here's the thing you must always remember about yourself: whatever it is that awaits you on this journey ahead, you will be strong and you will be brave. Your circumstances may not have changed but my friend you are no longer the same, you have grown in strength despite all your weaknesses.

HOLD ONTO YOU

And if you are overwhelmed
with the worries of the day
and stressed by the thoughts on
what might happen next,
remember that even in your
most painful of days
your heart is full of bravery,
courage and strength.
And even if it takes time
to make it through,
keep on believing in yourself,
keep on holding onto you.

SOMETHING MORE

You don't have to run away from the difficult. You don't have to fear the unknown. You can rest in the arms of hope. You can hold onto the light still shining inside you. You can start anew right where you are at this moment. You can trust in the voice in your heart that says, "there is something better, something more, waiting for you at the other end."

IN CASE NO ONE
HAS TOLD YOU THIS LATELY
YOU HAVE DONE A GREAT JOB
IN HOLDING ONTO YOURSELF
THROUGH ALL THESE DIFFICULTIES.

W H E N   I N   D O U B T

Trust that things will work out
maybe not exactly the way you have planned
but in the way they are best for you.
Even though what is best for you
will not always make sense to you,
your job is to keep going anyway
knowing that your life
will not be defined by your difficult days.

WHEN THINGS ARE HARD

When things are hard and you feel like you cannot go on any further from here, remind yourself of this: sometimes it's the difficult that brings out the best in you and shows your truest strength. But you have to believe in yourself more than what your circumstances tell you in order to grow and make progress. You cannot let the difficult turns in your journey stop you from moving forward, from fighting for the life you truly deserve.

THINGS WILL FALL INTO PLACE

You are not falling behind; you are not losing your way just because this season you are taking some time to slow down and rest. In your heart there are doubts and there are questions you don't have answers to. But it does not mean you are not progressing; you are not growing into the person you are meant to. Have faith in your journey and keep doing your best. And even though right now life is testing your patience and strength, trust that in their own time things in your life will fall into place.

NO MATTER HOW DIFFICULT
THINGS HAVE BEEN IN THE PAST,
TRUST THAT BEAUTIFUL THINGS
CAN STILL HAPPEN FROM HERE.

YOU ARE STILL HERE

I cannot tell you how long you still have to go through what you are going through, but I can tell you that in your own way you are going to make it through. And even if this season you do not feel that you are making any progress, the fact that you are still here and trying your best, is a sign of your bravery, courage and strength.

TO THE STRUGGLING

I know things have been difficult lately and no one has told you that you are capable of making through it. But no matter what has happened, your struggles are not going in vain. One day you will look back and see along the way you were becoming stronger, growing into the person you were meant to be.

SEASON OF CHANGE

I know this is a season of change
and overwhelming stress
but I hope you will look through
your difficulties
and find a reason to stay.
I hope you will choose to keep going
even if you do not make progress every single day.

LIFE

Life can be cruel and mean and hard on your heart sometimes. But you can still have the courage to be gentle with yourself, to be compassionate and kind on those days when things are hard and everything seems to weigh too much on your heart. You can still have the strength to rise through it, you can choose to love who you are. Remember, your life is more than what you go through, you are worth more than what life has made you feel you deserve.

REMINDER TO SELF

Today, instead of doubting yourself trust that even if you do not control anything else, you are still capable of doing your best. Instead of doubting your strength, remind yourself that you have been through challenges before and you will find your way through them again.

LIFE IS STILL BEAUTIFUL,
YOU ARE STILL WORTHY
NO MATTER WHAT HAPPENS
YOU ARE GOING TO GET THROUGH THIS.

GENTLE REMINDER

Gentle reminder that this season of pain and unexpected change is simply a part of your journey, no matter how permanent and never-ending they may seem right now. We all go through many phases of life as we grow; trust that these difficult days are also one of those phases of your growth. And just as they are hard and painful beyond measure, they are also great reminders of the strength and courage you possess in your heart. Remember: one day you will get through them and you will be thankful for the way they have made you strong.

FAITH

Wherever you are,
no matter what you are going through,
your life has value
and no matter how you feel
about your circumstances,
your struggles are not going in vain.
You may not feel joyous and hopeful
every single day
but you are still moving ahead,
you are making progress,
even if you can't see it yet.

RESILIENCE

I hope you will not start thinking less of yourself just because this year you could not make much progress. I hope you will be proud of yourself for still trying your best. It was not easy for you to make it even here and perhaps this year you have realized how powerful it is just to hang in there.

EVEN IN THE HOURS OF
STRANGENESS AND UNCERTAINTY,
MAY YOU NEVER FEEL AFRAID
TO HOLD SPACE FOR SOMETHING
BEAUTIFUL AND EXTRAORDINARY.

EMBRACE YOUR UNIQUENESS

When your heart is troubled with fear and doubts, when you are the only one seems to be different than others in the crowd, when you are not growing the way people around you are growing, be gentle with your heart and let it hold onto what is actually true: your journey is different than that of others and your uniqueness is your beauty and not a scar on your path. Remember - where you are today will not define what kind of a life you deserve.

NOTE TO SELF

And it is okay
if today was a day that did not go your way,
hanging in there and doing your best
are more than enough some days.

IF IT STILL HURTS

If it still hurts your heart because you have given so much to it and it still didn't work out, remember that there will be setbacks and failures along this journey but they will never define your worth. And even if you do not understand it, trust that there is purpose in this waiting, no matter how tiring and difficult it may seem right now.

NO MATTER HOW YOU FEEL

YOU ARE NOT ALONE IN ALL OF THIS,

EVEN IF IT DOESN'T MAKE SENSE TODAY,

EVEN IF IT TAKES TIME TO GET THROUGH THIS.

CHANGING THINGS

While you wait
to make sense of changing things
I hope you will not stop moving ahead
and trying new things.
You may not know everything yet
but you are still here
and there is time for you
to get to where you need to be.

Dhiman

EVEN IN YOUR DIFFICULT DAYS
YOU ARE ALLOWED TO
WALK THROUGH THINGS
IN YOUR OWN TIME AND PACE.

<u>H O P E</u>

Be hopeful. Be brave. I know a lot of things in your life have changed and almost none of them will ever be the same but despite all that has happened, you are still you my friend and you have come a long way through all the storms that life put in your way. And even though they seemed difficult at that moment, you believed that you are strong enough to overcome them.

BECOMING

Maybe you are stressed
and you are struggling
and deep down
there is pain in your heart
that you are carrying
but even here along this long
and restless journey
my friend you are becoming
who you are meant to be.

I HOPE YOU WILL NEVER
SEE YOURSELF UNWORTHY
JUST BECAUSE YOU COULDN'T BECOME
WHAT SOMEONE ELSE WANTED YOU TO BE.

Dhiman

Strong Enough

Dhiman

THE JOURNEY

Strong Enough

Dhiman

STRONG

It is okay if your 'strong'
looks different every day.
Some days it means
being courageous and brave,
some days it means slowing down
and healing yourself
but no matter what it looks like,
remember it is enough
even if it doesn't feel that way sometimes.

THE JOURNEY

When you began walking on this journey, you did not know where you were heading or where you would end up someday. You did not know how far you could go and the roadblocks along the way made your heart more worried and stressed. All you had was hope and the choice to keep going anyway. And now years later as you look back on the journey, I hope you feel proud of the way you have handled the not-so-easy days. I hope you see the purpose in all that has happened and be grateful for how far you have come along the way.

YOU ARE NO LONGER THE SAME YOU
YOU HAVE COME SO FAR
AND YOU HAVE MADE IT THROUGH
DESPITE ALL THAT HAS HAPPENED
THERE IS SOMETHING BRAVE
AND BEAUTIFUL ABOUT YOU.

FINDING STRENGTH

This year you have learned to trust yourself. You have seen strength rising through your most difficult days. You have been hurt and there were days when you were falling apart but you have held onto yourself, you did not give up on your heart. And despite all the hurdles on your path, you have managed to come this far.

REASONS

As much as there are reasons to be afraid,
there are also reasons to be hopeful,
to keep on walking
even in the unknown,
to know that you are worthy
and you belong.

THINGS I HOPE FOR YOU

I hope you will walk on this journey knowing that you belong. I hope even if things sometimes do not go your way you will not stop trying, you will not give up on yourself. And on your toughest days I hope you will keep reminding yourself of this: you are loved and you are worthy, even when it doesn't feel that way.

RESTART

Keep believing in life's possibility to change. Believe in your own self too. Maybe times are still hard for you and you don't know how you are going to make it through another year with a broken heart. Maybe you are going through things you never thought you would have to. But even in the difficult, there is opportunity for you to restart. Trust that one day things will change and what hurts you so much today will also be your source of strength.

FOR THE ONE
EMBARKING ON A NEW PATH

The road ahead will be new
and maybe you are afraid of
what it might hold for you,
but here's the truth
that you must always hold onto:
as much as there is uncertainty
on this journey
there will also be opportunities
for you to grow,
to embrace who you are,
to love yourself more.

HANG IN THERE

Maybe this season you had more bad days than good ones. But even in all of this be brave enough to keep moving forward. Remember life doesn't stay the same for too long, it somehow finds a way to change. Your bad days will not go away suddenly but one day the good ones will outnumber them. Hang in there, hold onto yourself. You will find a way.

MAKING ROOM IN YOUR HEART

It is true that not every person you meet along this journey will belong to you and many of them will never hold in their heart a place for you. But I just hope you know that even though it will hurt you, it will never define your worth. Believe that you will find love and friendship again, in places you will least expect. You will find people who will look into your heart and love you as you are. All I hope is that you will not give up on love and you will not be afraid of letting some people go along this journey in order to make room for the ones who are truly worthy of your heart.

Dhiman

LEARNING TO TAKE IT DAY BY DAY
DOESN'T MAKE YOU WEAK ANY WAY.

<u>Y O U   H A V E   M A D E   I T   H E R E</u>

Think about all the things that worried your heart this time last year. Think about how you have managed to hold onto hope despite all your fears. So many things used to bother you but none of them have turned out to be true. And even though you were not sure where you will be this year, you have made it through all your struggles and fears, you have made it here.

YOU WILL MAKE MISTAKES
AND YOU WILL FALL DOWN SOME DAYS
BUT I HOPE YOU KNOW
THEY WILL NEVER MAKE YOU
WORTH ANY LESS.

Y O U   A R E   W O R T H Y

Even if no one has ever told you this,
I hope you will always remember –
you are worthy even in your difficulties.
This is a season that has tested you for too long
and I know it's not been easy for you
to keep holding on
but here you are my friend,
brave and strong,
keep going despite it all.

Dhiman

BELIEVE IN YOURSELF

Trust the journey, believe in yourself. The biggest strength you can ever possess is the strength of loving and believing in yourself. There will be times in your life when the path will be long, uncertain and difficult. You will feel unsure if you will ever be able to make it through. But when you believe in yourself, no matter how hard the journey gets you know you have the strength to get through it anyway.

JUST BECAUSE

Just because someone has given up on you
I hope you will not give up on yourself.
When life hands you difficult days
I hope you choose to be gentle with yourself.
Life will not always go the way you plan,
there will be failures and heartbreaks along the way
but they will make you strong
and you will grow anyway.

Dhiman

YOU ARE ENOUGH

You are not your difficult days. You are not your past mistakes. You are not what you failed at. You are not what others said you are. You are more than the opinions of others. You are stronger than you think you are. You have come this far and no longer where you once were. Even though life is still hard, you are doing your best and that is what really matters.

LOVING THE SELF

Do not treat yourself in a way that belittles all the progress you have made along this journey. Be kind to yourself. Keep room in your life for falling downs and making mistakes. Honor your past self, prepare for your future self but remember to take care of who you are today. Be grateful for what you have. Be hopeful no matter how hard things get and remember to do your best even if that means just to survive some days.

REASONS TO BE HOPEFUL

Never let the difficult
take you away from the truth
that even when it's not easy,
even when it's not all bright and beautiful,
there is still room for you to be hopeful.
For it is more than okay
to go through days that are slow
and not filled with progress,
to get so close to your dreams
and still feeling scared of things
not going your way.
But through it all my friend,
I hope you will keep on moving ahead,
believing in yourself.

EVEN HERE

THERE ARE MOMENTS OF HOPE

AND THERE IS ALSO LIGHT

LEADING YOU INTO NEW DOORS.

Dhiman

YOU WILL FIND YOUR WAY

Even if you find yourself
struggling to make a way
out of these uncertain days,
remember you are strong and brave,
you are still capable of doing your best.
Some days the pain will be too deep
and the only answer you will have
is carrying on anyway.
But you will be okay,
despite it all my friend,
you will find your way.

N O T E   T O   S E L F

Go easy on yourself today. Be a little more kind to who you are. If you are feeling sad and all of this seems strange right now, know that it's okay. It's okay to feel uncertain and different and not have every aspect of your life figured out. In time you will learn what you need to learn, you will do what you need to do. But for today, do what feels right for your heart and you.

LET IT BE THE SEASON
YOU LEARN TO SAY TO YOURSELF:
"I'M WORTHY, I'M ENOUGH,
I'M PROUD OF HOW FAR I HAVE COME."

LESSON IN THE DIFFICULT

Do not let your failures decide what you deserve in life. No matter how many times you fall down in life, always have the courage to get up and try. Things will be hard sometimes. No, you will not be able to do everything right all the time. But you will learn as you go, through your mistakes and falling downs and one day you will see that your past did not define your whole life.

TO DO:

SLOW DOWN OFTEN
COUNT YOUR BLESSINGS
BE KIND TO YOUR HEART
BELIEVE IN NEW BEGINNINGS

ONE STEP AT A TIME

Do what is possible for you right now. Take small steps towards what seems hard from here. Take your time to figure things out if things do not go your way, but please do not give up on yourself just because you are having a hard day. Face the difficult and the unknown with courage and know that courage could mean hanging onto yourself some days.

WAITING

Through the roadblocks and difficult days,
through the mountaintops and unknown ways,
you have survived through it all
and you have always found a way.
So even here if your circumstances do not change
and for a little while you still have to wait,
remember the journey you have already made
and be grateful for how far you have come,
today and every day.

A REMINDER

It's okay if all of this was too heavy for your heart
and to process it you needed more time than you
anticipated. Please don't be hard on yourself for
feeling things deeply. Remember you are a human
being and feeling your feelings is what gives you
true freedom and strength.

PERHAPS THIS SEASON
IS NOT ABOUT MEETING SOMEONE NEW
BUT MORE ABOUT YOU MEETING
YOUR OWN INNER SELF IN A NEW WAY.

CHANGE

Not everyday
is meant to take you forward,
some are simply there to remind you:
it is okay to go through slow and stagnant days,
and even though it is hurting,
it will not always stay the same.

LET THIS SEASON OF STRUGGLE
BE A REMINDER THAT
LIKE EVERYTHING BRAVE AND
BEAUTIFUL IN THE WILD
YOUR HEART WILL GROW IN ITS OWN TIME.

GROW IN YOUR OWN WAY

There's no outgrowing one another. You don't have to follow the footsteps of someone else in order to grow and make progress, to be who you are meant to be. You don't have to grow in a certain way in order to have value on this earth. Your job is to be you and to grow in your own way without comparing your journey with anyone else. So be gentle with yourself, love who you are no matter what stage of growth you are going through at the moment. You might still have a long way to go but how far you have come in this journey of growth, still matters so much.

PATH OF YOUR DREAMS

You may have missed
a lot of things
but I hope you know my friend
you are not alone in all of this.
Perhaps waiting in this season
seems longer than it has ever been,
you are still here
moving slowly and gently
along the path of your dreams.

IN THE END

Remember: in the end it's not others but what you think about yourself that really matters. Do not be afraid of choosing a life that is best for you. Do not hesitate to make a change that might upset someone but allows you to get one step closer to your dreams. There is no easy way to get to the life you want but one way of making it more difficult is to let others decide what you deserve in life.

THE BRAVEST THING
YOU WILL EVER DO
IS CHOOSING TO LOVE YOURSELF
WHEN NO ONE ELSE IS CHOOSING YOU.

A STRONGER YOU

Remember where you were a week, a month or a year ago. Notice how you have overcome the obstacles time and time again. A lot of things have changed along the way and you have changed as well. But within you there is something new, a new hope is rising through. With belief, bravery and courage, you are learning to build a stronger you.

THROUGH LIFE'S HIGHS AND THE LOWS
AND THE DAYS THAT HURT YOU THE MOST,
I HOPE YOU WILL TRUST YOUR STRENGTH,
YOU WILL BE BRAVE ENOUGH
TO LOVE YOURSELF.

NEW START

Believe that you have what you need in order to build the life you want. Trust that no matter what went wrong in the past, you are capable of doing things right this time.

TO HOPE

IS NOT TO ESCAPE THE DIFFICULT

BUT TO BE ABLE TO

MOVE FORWARD WITH COURAGE

DESPITE THE DIFFICULT.

TO BE STRONG AND BRAVE

To go through hard days,
through the unknown and the uncertain,
to feel hurt and get heartbroken
over and over again
and still choosing to go on
without losing hope for better days –
that is what it means to be strong,
that is what it means to be brave.

Dhiman

Strong Enough

Dhiman

KEEP GOING

Strong Enough

Dhiman

KEEP GOING

If you don't feel hopeful for the future that you are moving towards and wondering if there's anything to look forward, remember the good that also happened to you along this journey and not just the things that were difficult. Yes, there were phases of this journey that were hard and a lot of times it felt like your struggles will never end but through it all you have seen that in your heart there is strength, and there is always hope if you keep on going, if you dare to believe in the life you are worthy of.

SOMEONE ELSE'S PROGRESS
DOES NOT MAKE YOURS ANY LESS.

PURPOSE

Maybe all of this is meant to guide you to a place where you are truly loved, needed and belong. Maybe the right time, the right door is just around the corner and no matter what struggles you are going through right now, you can hold onto the hope that you are going to make it through somehow.

CONNECTING THE DOTS

There were times in your life when you did not feel ready and you thought you were not good enough. There were seasons that hardly went your way. There were feelings that weighed too heavy on your heart. And if you still have days that make you doubt your worth, remember: no matter what went wrong or what seemed unconquerable in the past, you have made it through, your hardships did not define your worth.

MAY YOU MEASURE YOUR PROGRESS
BY HOW FAR YOU HAVE COME,
NOT BY HOW FAR AHEAD
OTHERS ARE FROM YOU.

N E W   Y O U

Each day in tiny, countless and sometimes unnoticeable ways you are growing and evolving into a better version of your past self. It's okay if not all your days are filled with visible progress. Some days you just have to sit down and spend time with yourself, appreciating how much you have grown and how far you have come along the way.

POSSIBILITIES

I know things have been hard
and many things in your life
did not go your way in the past
but you can still take heart
in the truth that somehow
you have managed to survive
through all the pain and hurt.
This is a new season of possibilities
and I hope you know my friend
with hope and courage in your heart
you are capable of making
something beautiful out of it.

INVEST IN YOURSELF

Invest in yourself. Learn to let go of anything or anyone that wants to go and instead, make space for people and things worth holding on. You don't have to keep on carrying the old life you have already left behind. Embrace your new life, the life you have right now. Even here, I know some things will not be easy but you will be strong enough to get through them. Maybe not today and that's okay. The most beautiful thing about life is how it offers you another chance, a new day to start living all over again.

STRONG ENOUGH

There is still strength within the depths of your heart even if it doesn't seem that way where you are right now. Know that when things fall apart, they leave you exactly where you need to start again. You don't have to feel strong every single day in order to overcome your challenges. Just knowing that you are still here and doing your best with what you have is enough to make it through some days.

B E L I E F

Maybe the heartbreak you went through is still fresh, the memories are too many and the pain is too deep. Maybe it is starting to feel like eternity with no hope in sight. But remember, this is how we are supposed to feel when parts of us are lost with someone we loved with all of our being. It's never easy to keep going when you are hurting inside. Please give your heart the time it needs, do not rush it. One day you will get through this, you'll outgrow all these things that are holding you back right now. Trust that you are capable and strong enough and even though it is difficult, believe that through this season life is leading you to the things you are worthy of.

NO MATTER

No matter how hard it was on you,
know that today was not a waste.
You may not have made much progress
but still you have managed
to show up and did your best.
Give yourself credit for surviving this day.

LETTING GO

There are times in life when holding onto some things takes you away from the life you are truly worthy of. Sometimes the only choice you will have is to let go and trust and see where life takes you. I know it's not easy, this trusting in the unknown, this carrying on in a dark and never-ending path. But you will find out along the way that even though it is hard, it is also full of wonderful opportunities if you are willing to endure through those temporary moments of difficult, if you are brave enough to choose the life you deserve.

IT IS OKAY TO SAY 'I'M NOT OKAY'
AND 'I NEED MORE TIME
TO GET THROUGH THESE DAYS.'
A LOT OF TIMES IN LIFE
THINGS WILL NOT MAKE ANY SENSE
AND IT IS OKAY FOR YOU TO TAKE YOUR TIME
TO NAVIGATE THROUGH THOSE PHASES.

START WHERE YOU ARE

No, you can't change everything. But I hope you know this: you are always capable of new beginnings. Some losses in life can be devastating, heart-breaking and painful beyond measure but there is so much more to your life than what is no longer by your side. Reach out and open your heart to the possibilities of life. Start today in small steps, start where you are.

THERE WILL BE A DAY
WHEN YOU WILL LOOK BACK
ON YOUR JOURNEY AND SAY:
THE HARD DAYS HAVE TESTED MY STRENGTH
BUT I'M STILL HERE
AND I'VE NOT GIVEN UP ON MYSELF.

EVEN IN YOUR HARD DAYS

THROUGH ALL THAT HAS HAPPENED

AND DID NOT HAPPEN

YOU HAVE COME THIS FAR

AND THAT IS A BRAVE

AND BEAUTIFUL THING

MY FRIEND.

FRIEND

Be that friend to yourself who says, "even though the journey ahead will not be easy, you will still be okay, you will find a way through it."

HOW FAR YOU HAVE COME

Consider how far and impossible it all seemed in the beginning. Consider the doubts and worries you had in your heart when you were going through hardships, the times you felt like there will never be an end to your pain. And while there are things you still need to go through as you continue walking on this unknown and untraveled path, may you notice how far you have already come, how strong you have been in all that you had to overcome.

EVEN IF YOU ARE OVERWHELMED
BY EVERYTHING THAT IS
HAPPENING AROUND YOU,
MAY YOU KEEP FAITH IN YOUR HEART
THAT YOUR JOURNEY IS STILL
GOING TO UNFOLD
IN THE WAY THAT IS BEST FOR YOU.

HEALING

Things have changed and everything you once held so close to your heart may have fallen apart and I know their memories still hurt you some days. But every single day you are making peace with your pain, you are learning to be gentle with your heart again.

STRENGTH

If the only thing you can do right now is survive,
do that. Trust that in this difficult time
this is what strength looks like.

TAKE YOUR TIME

Do not let the difficult parts of your life harden your heart. Be gentle with yourself, be loving and kind. Remember there's so much more to your life than what you had to leave behind. Be hopeful and brave and see how every obstacle you have faced on this journey has somehow made you strong along the way. So even here if doubts still creep into your mind, remind your worried self that it's okay to feel this way, it's okay to take your time.

DOUBTS

If today is making you doubt your strength, remind yourself of all the things you have overcome along the way. Today, instead of fearing what is ahead, let your heart be guided by faith. Remember: whatever you are facing today is simply a test of your resilience, of how bravely you can carry on despite things not going your way.

NEW BEGINNINGS

Have hope for new beginnings. Whatever the past has done to you, it need not determine what the future holds for you. No matter what pain you had to go through this time last year, remember you no longer belong there. You have been bruised and you have been hurt but despite it all, you have come so far. And I hope you know you are good enough to start again to pursue the life you are worthy of, right where you are today.

YEAR OF UNCERTAINTY

It has been a year of chaos and uncertainty
and while it was easy for you to give up,
you chose to continue moving forward.
And one day at a time with courage and trust,
you have made it through my friend,
you have come this far.

STRONGEST WAY

You are strong and brave
and I hope you notice
how you have overcome
the highs and the lows of life
through the unknown
and uncertain days
and even though
the roadblocks did not change,
you have changed my friend
in the strongest of ways.

PURPOSE IN YOUR STRUGGLES

I hope you are doing well. I hope even in the midst of every pain, difficulty and chaos you are committing yourself to be a little more kind and gentle with your heart. I know life can be more than difficult sometimes but I hope you are finding the strength to keep on going even on those days. I hope things are changing for you and you are starting to see the purpose and the good in all that you have been through.

ON MOVING FORWARD

As you move forward in life, remember this: it will not always be the way you want it to be. There will be ups and downs and there will also be days of pain and setbacks. But if you keep on doing your best without worrying about what's going to happen in the end, you will see that the very thing that scared you someday have made you stronger along the way and what you thought to be the end was in fact life's way of telling you that there is more to your life than what you thought you deserve.

GRATITUDE

So many things around you have changed this year and while you still need time to make sense of everything, remember that there were also things that stood by you through it all and that my friend, is something to be grateful for.

BRAVING THE UNKNOWN

When you walked into this season of change, there were so many things you did not know about yourself. You did not know your strength; you did not know that what you were going through would matter so much someday. But as you continued moving ahead, you have learned to see the light through the darkness, you have braved the unknown and you have grown in strength. And even though your courage did not mean much that day, it is what has brought you where you are today.

SOMETIMES

Sometimes things do not go your way even if you do your best. Sometimes things need more time than you anticipate. You cannot change everything that happens to you but you can always choose to learn from them, grow and become a stronger and a better version of yourself.

REASONS TO KEEP GOING

Give yourself love. Give yourself compassion and kindness. Life can be strange and difficult and beyond your understanding some days. But it is still beautiful and worthy and there are reasons for you to keep going anyway. Even if you do not know the purpose of certain things that have happened to you along the way, trust that one day it will all make sense. Maybe your life will not change all of a sudden but that does not mean what you are going through will never change. Give life the time it needs to prepare you for better things. Give your heart the time it needs to grow through these circumstances.

START TODAY. START IN SMALL STEPS.
MAYBE YOU WILL NOT GET TOO FAR
AND MAYBE YOU WILL FALL DOWN AGAIN.
BUT EVERY DAY IN TRYING YOUR BEST
YOU WILL ALSO FIND YOUR TRUEST STRENGTH.

TO THE ARTIST IN YOU

Make art for yourself. For the world. For the love of creation. It's okay if only a few likes it. It's okay if no one likes it. Keep doing your thing. You may not save the world from falling apart but you can give someone hope through your art and who knows you might save someone's life. Isn't that enough on a day when life feels too heavy, too difficult?

PROCESS

We have to keep living regardless of what is going on around us. No matter what we go through in life, every single day brings a different experience. Some days we thrive, some days we just learn to survive. There is no perfect way to live this life. There is only doing our own individual best. And that best might look different every day and that is okay. As long as we are here and trying our best, we are doing alright and we will always find a way.

Strong Enough

Dhiman